NEWFOUNDLAND

OUR NORTH DOOR NEIGHBOR

NEWFOUNDLAND

OUR NORTH DOOR NEIGHBOR

By

A. C. SHELTON

ILLUSTRATED WITH PHOTOGRAPHS BY THE AUTHOR

1941

E. P. DUTTON & CO., INC.

NEW YORK

PRINTED IN THE U.S.A.

First Edition

LIST OF ILLUSTRATIONS

LIST OF ILLUSTRATIONS

LIST OF ILLUSTRATIONS

LIST OF ILLUSTRATIONS

IN GRATEFUL ACKNOWLEDGMENT

I offer this word of appreciation, especially to the Newfoundland Tourist and Publicity Commission and the Newfoundland Railway, through their respective officials C. C. Duley and H. J. Russell. Their intense interest and active support made the gathering of this series of photographic studies possible. Without their help I would not have been able to reach and photograph many of the regions presented.

I am indebted also to a man who proved to be a real friend during many long days spent on the trails and down the rivers and across the lakes: R. Mosdell, of the Newfoundland Railway staff—"Dick" to all his host of friends, a veteran huntsman even back to the days of abundant caribou, a master fisherman intimately acquainted with every river and lake, every nook and corner of this Great Island. No photographer afield ever had a better companion.

Also I acknowledge with real appreciation the kindly assistance of H. M. Maddick of St. John's, who so ably piloted me here, there and everywhere over the Avalon Peninsula.

And last, but by no means least, my gratitude to that host of friendly Newfoundlanders—whether employees of the Railway, owners of hunting and fishing camps and lodges, guides and packers on the trails, Indian guides with their battered service-worn canoes and their uncanny, unerring accuracy in piloting their heavily laden frail craft down swift waters, or fisherfolk at their daily tasks in the fishing villages along the coast—who were each and every one so willing to help me in any way.

To all the kindly folk above, *Newfoundland: Our North Door Neighbor* owes its existence.

Thank you, one and all.

A. C. Shelton

NEWFOUNDLAND

OUR NORTH DOOR NEIGHBOR

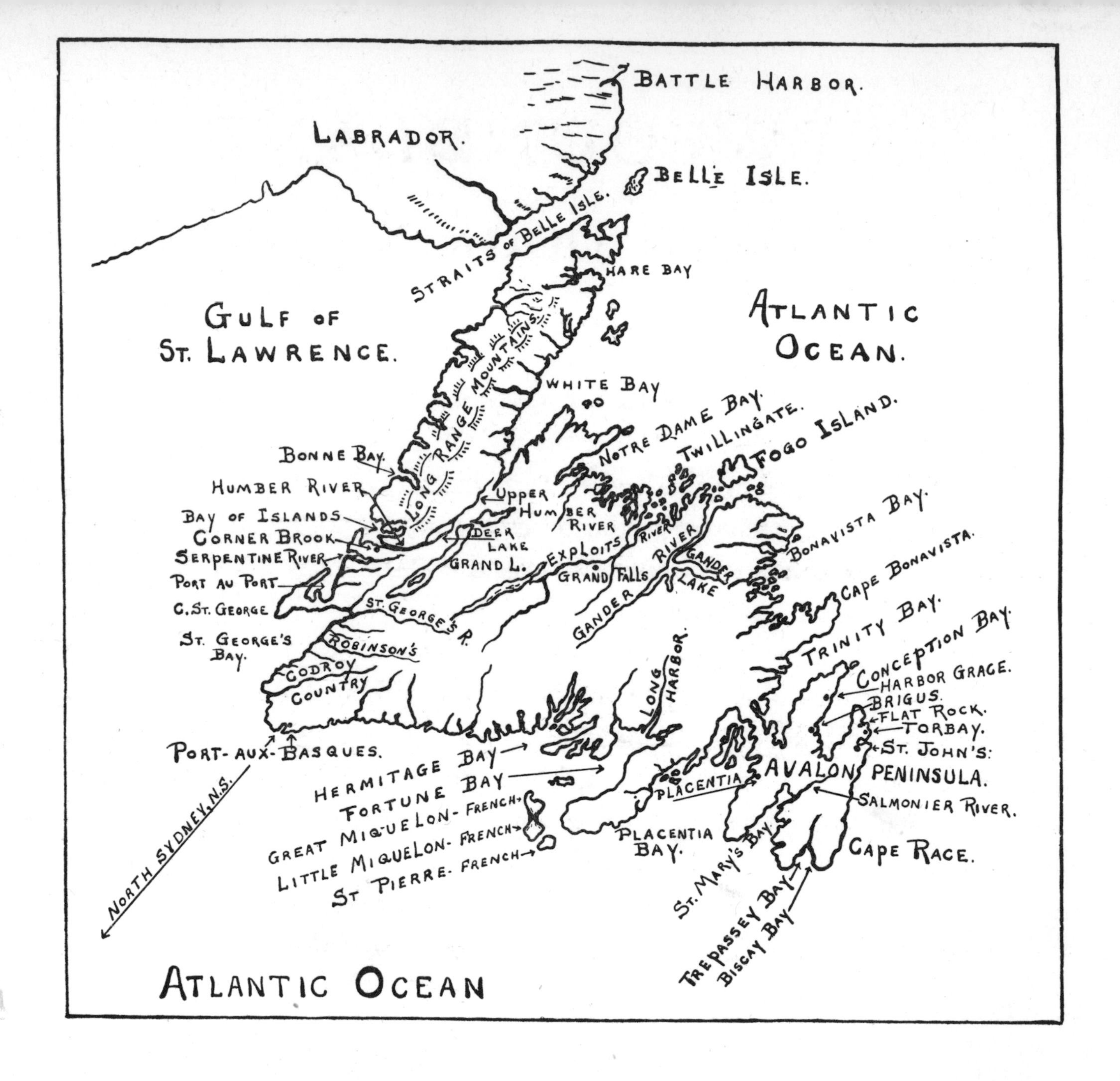

Battle Harbor.
Labrador.
Belle Isle.
Straits of Belle Isle.
Hare Bay
Gulf of St. Lawrence.
Atlantic Ocean.
Long Range Mountains
White Bay
Notre Dame Bay.
Twillingate.
Fogo Island.
Bonne Bay.
Humber River
Bay of Islands
Corner Brook
Serpentine River
Port au Port
C. St. George
St. George's Bay.
Upper Humber River
Deer Lake
Grand L.
Exploits River
Grand Falls
Gander River
Gander Lake
Bonavista Bay.
Cape Bonavista.
St. George's R.
Robinson's
Codroy Country
Trinity Bay.
Conception Bay.
Harbor Grace.
Brigus.
Flat Rock.
Torbay.
St. John's.
Long Harbor.
Port-aux-Basques.
Hermitage Bay
Fortune Bay
Great Miquelon - French
Little Miquelon - French
St Pierre - French
Placentia
Avalon Peninsula.
Salmonier River.
Placentia Bay.
St. Mary's Bay.
Cape Race.
Trepassey Bay
Biscay Bay
North Sydney, N.S.
Atlantic Ocean

NEWFOUNDLAND

OUR NORTH DOOR NEIGHBOR

TO THE HARDY, ADVENTUROUS SEAMEN OF WESTERN EUROPE, WHO EXPLORED THESE SHORES a hundred years and more before the British planted a colony at Jamestown, Virginia, Newfoundland was indeed a "New-Found-Land."

It is Britain's oldest colony, and its discovery, its history and settlement, its growth and development are inseparably linked with the early history and the later colonization of North America.

John Cabot, early explorer, discovered Newfoundland in 1497, only five years after Columbus' discovery of the New World. John Cabot was not hunting for Newfoundland. He was seeking the Northwest Passage to India, on which mission he had sailed from Bristol, England, in May, 1497. His vessel of discovery was *The Goode Ship Matthewe,* manned by a worthy crew of fearless, hardy, and adventurous seamen. Cabot is generally believed to have landed at Cape Bonavista, on the rugged and beautiful northeast coast, north of Trinity Bay. Claiming this "New-Found-Land" by right of discovery, Cabot raised aloft the flag of Britain, and prevailed upon King Henry the Seventh to grant him a charter in order that he might carry still further his explorations and discoveries in the name of the Crown.

Word of the discovery and of the amazing wealth and vast resources of this "New-Found-Land" spread rapidly throughout Western Europe. The rich fishing grounds along the northeast shores of this newly discovered world had long been known to the hardy fishermen from Portugal and the Bay of Biscay. It was only natural, therefore, following the discovery of the land by Cabot, that the English, Portuguese, and Basque fishermen should begin to voyage in ever-increasing numbers to these fabulously rich new fishing waters, with the French and Spanish soon following. In a short while, so many ships were sailing these newly discovered seas that by 1522 the British Admiralty was forced to send armed vessels to meet the laden fishing fleet on its way home and to give it convoy protection from raiding French privateers, whose bold piracy constitutes a fascinating—if lawless—chapter of the early history of our northeast shores.

The influence and the imprint of early discovery was deeply written into the soil of Newfoundland during the one-hundred-year period between 1500 and 1600—and written in by many lands. Today the very names of her cities and towns and the coastal outports bear witness to this early contact with the Old World. Bacalieu, Port-Aux-Basques, Biscay Arm, Spaniard Bay, Harbour Breton, Portugal

Cove, English Harbour, Frenchmen's Arm, Bay de Verde, Trepassey Bay, St. Pierre, Cape Miquelon, and many others, are today commonplace names on any Newfoundland map, names that bear long witness to the exploration, conquest and settlement of the "New-Found-Land" of John Cabot, by the British, the French, the Portuguese, the Spanish and the Basques.

Dominant from the beginning, the English were in the great majority. The first colonial government was set up in 1583. Letters patent had been granted by Queen Elizabeth to Sir Humphrey Gilbert, a half-brother of Sir Walter Raleigh. Anchored in St. John's harbor—even then famous as the center of the fishing industry in this newly discovered empire—Sir Humphrey read these letters patent, and thus established the first colonial government in the British Dominions. St. John's, therefore, has the double distinction of being not only the oldest city in North America (founded in 1503), but the first British Dominion capital, outside of Great Britain proper.

In the years that followed, exploration by the French became active and intense. Jacques Cartier, intrepid seaman of St. Malo, France, made his famous voyage of exploration to the coast of Newfoundland in 1534. He came again, in 1535-1536, and still again in 1541-1543. Discoverer of the great St. Lawrence River, his name is inseparably linked with the creation of the French colonial empire in North America.

Realizing the potential wealth of these newly discovered lands, France determined to colonize them in her own behalf. She sent over another personage well known in the discovery history of the period, Champlain, who arrived in 1603. But, devoting his energies to exploration in what is now the Province of Quebec, Champlain did not land on Newfoundland soil at that time. The French, nonetheless, had established by 1660 a capital at Placentia, a strategic point on Placentia Bay, on the southern coast of Newfoundland—away to the south and southwest of St. John's. Here they fortified their position, and in the following years made attack after attack on the English settlements. So strongly were they established and so intense were these attacks that the British capital, St. John's, was captured and retaken no less than three times. This continual strife, however, was settled by the Treaty of Utrecht, 1713, by the terms of which treaty France gave up all claims to Newfoundland proper, but she was permitted to engage in fishing and the drying of fish on the southern and western coasts. As a natural result, the French became firmly established in these areas, especially upon the islands of St. Pierre and Miquelon, a short distance off the southeast tip of Newfoundland. St. Pierre and Miquelon still remain in the possession of France.

Today, the hardy descendants of these early settlers inhabit the shores of the Great Island and its towns and villages inland. Here you find a sturdy, industrious people—happy, kindly, hospitable—regardless of whether the blood that courses through their veins traces backward through the generations to British, or Basque, to French or Portuguese, or Spanish. Today they are Newfoundlanders all, a kindly folk who ask but little in return for their hard labors and the manifold tasks that confront them in their never-ending struggle to wrest a livelihood from sea and shore, and forest—a folk whom to know is to love, honor and respect!

So much has been written, so much has been spoken, portraying Newfoundland as cold, bleak and barren, as a semi-frozen land of iceberg and impoverished Eskimo, that I hope I may, in some small measure, counter this wrong impression, so unfair to a beautiful land of majestic coastal scenery, of dense forests, of grand lakes and magnificent rivers, and of kind-hearted people.

Like "all Gaul," Newfoundland is *in tres partes divisa*. Eastward lies the Avalon Peninsula, nearly cut off to form a separate island by itself, where the great arm of Trinity Bay reaches down from the north almost to meet the equally long arm of Placentia Bay, coming up from the south. At the point where they so nearly meet, a narrow neck of land forms the isthmus which joins the Avalon Peninsula to what I think of as the great central body of Newfoundland proper. While there is some forest area on the Avalon Peninsula, it is not so heavily forested as the western parts of the Island. The Avalon Peninsula is particularly a region of high rocky cliffs, spectacular marine scenery and majestic ocean. Many areas are barren and rocky, covered with sparse vegetation, where blueberries and wild strawberries grow in abundance. These rocky, rolling regions are what are spoken of universally throughout the Island as the "barrens." These "barrens" also extend partially across the northern area of central Newfoundland, giving way to the region of dense forests, as one approaches the west coast.

Westward from Trinity and Placentia bays extends this great body of central Newfoundland, to the regions of Red Indian Lake, Grand Lake, and the Humber River country. This is a vast expanse of rolling, undulating terrain, of dense, heavy forests, innumerable rivers, countless lakes, and of rocky, barren and swampy "tundra." Much of this area was formerly the home and the haunt of the vast herds of caribou that ranged far and wide in their migrations from north to south—and from south to north. Much of this area is still virgin land, trackless and, in part, treeless, its primitive natural beauty untouched and unspoiled.

The third great division of Newfoundland is the west coast. From the picturesque little coastal outport of Port-Aux-Basques, at the extreme southwestern tip of the Island, one travels up along the western coast through such beautiful valleys as the Little Codroy, and the Big Codroy. One crosses such rivers as Robinson's, Fischell's and the many other beautiful streams that flow down from the hills through heavy forest and lovely valley to empty into St. George's Bay.

To the north lies the region of Grand Lake, and, further on, the mighty Humber River rises near the head of White Bay to flow to the south and west, where it empties into the Gulf of St. Lawrence, through the long reach of Humber Arm, at Bay of Islands. North from there stretches the long arm of the northern peninsula of Newfoundland, reaching far up to the Straits of Belle Isle, directly across which lies the coast of Labrador. Extending the length of this northern arm, are the Long Range Mountains, an extremely beautiful mountain chain averaging some 2,000 feet in altitude, and in many places rising directly from the sea. Along this coast is to be found some of the most majestic scenery of the Island Dominion.

In its shape Newfoundland is, roughly, a great triangle, slightly over 300 miles from east to west, and the same distance from north to south. With an area of some 43,000 sq. miles, the Island has a coastline of over 4,000 miles. This entire coast, as is evident by a glance at any Newfoundland map, is deeply indented with countless bays and sheltered harbors. These range from tiny rocky inlets, through beautiful harbor bays such as Brigus, famous as the home of Captain Bob Bartlett, to the great harbor of St. John's itself, one of the finest landlocked harbors in the world. There is scarcely a straight stretch of any length on the entire coast, and the great bays of the Island indent its coast to a distance of forty or fifty miles, or even more.

While Newfoundland possesses countless rivers, three are of major importance. Probably the best known is the ever-famous Humber, mecca of salmon fishermen the world over. Rising to the northeast, the Humber flows southwest through the region of the Big Falls of the Humber, down between beautiful mountains clothed by dense forests. From these forests countless cords of pulpwood are drifted down on the waters of the Humber to the great paper mills at Corner Brook, and thence in the form of paper to the printing presses of England, Canada and the United States.

Gliding swiftly under the towering crag of Marblehead, the Humber widens out at the village of Humbermouth and proceeds through the long reach of Humber Arm to the Bay of Islands, which is in reality the scenic mouth of the Humber in the St. Lawrence Gulf.

Two other great rivers of the Island are the Exploits and the Gander. The Gander rises in central Newfoundland and flows northeast into vast Gander Lake and thence from Gander Lake north to empty into the sea at Gander Bay. Further to the southwest, in the region of Red Indian Lake, rises the Exploits River, also flowing northeast, into the Bay of Exploits, which bay in turn opens into Notre Dame Bay and so to the open North Atlantic Ocean.

In addition to these three great rivers, there are countless smaller ones, rising anywhere from a few to many miles inland from the coast, and flowing down into one or other of the innumerable bays that indent the shore. Many of these are beautiful streams and among them, especially, should be mentioned the Salmonier River of the Avalon Peninsula, the La Poile, on the south coast, the Little Codroy, the Big Codroy, St. George's and Harry's Rivers, and the spectacular Serpentine River on the west coast.

Known from early days as "The Land Where Cod Is King," fishing has always been the chief industry of the Island. Every seaport, every harbor, and every village along the coast is a fishing port, where cod is landed and cured in vast quantities. Over 70,000 tons of cod are cured and shipped from Newfoundland annually. Fishing is carried on in fishing boats and vessels of many kinds, and the fishing waters range from a few miles offshore to as far away as the Grand Banks and the Labrador coast. The coast of Labrador and the Banks are the area of greatest fishing activity. It is estimated that probably twenty percent of the population of Newfoundland are engaged in the fishing industry.

While fishing employs the largest number of individual workers, the industry does not rank first, however, in economic importance. From the standpoint of income and revenue, pulp and paper rank number one among industries in Newfoundland. Corner Brook and Grand Falls are the great paper centers of the Island. The innumerable cords of pulpwood annually converted into pulp and paper supply the markets of England, Canada and the United States.

There is considerable farming throughout Newfoundland, but agriculture as yet can scarcely be classed as an important industry, other than as supplying local needs. Throughout western Newfoundland, particularly, there are many fertile valleys which will undoubtedly some day blossom fruitfully under cultivation.

Another industry famous throughout the years in story and picture, but of lesser economic importance today, is the sealing industry. In years gone by, immense fleets of sealing vessels choked such harbors as St. John's and Brigus, and from these ports the great sealing fleets sailed early in the spring, to the vast ice fields where seals in their hundreds of thousands were taken and slain. Year by year, however, the sealing industry has dwindled, and today, as you stand upon the cliffs at Brigus and look down upon that quiet and peaceful harbor, there is no trace left of these sealing fleets of days gone by. In the harbor of St. John's you will find the few remaining remnants of this sealing fleet, riding at anchor, peacefully oblivious of the fierce activity of bygone days.

Destined eventually to become a great vacation land, the crying need of Newfoundland today is for roads and highways. Best known to tourists, the Avalon Peninsula and the region of St. John's offer a treasure house of scenic beauty, easily accessible to traveler and tourist. The city of St. John's is unique and picturesque, protected by its marvelous landlocked harbor and surrounded by high hills. Entrance to the harbor is through the Narrows, a cleft in the rocky shore, so narrow that in olden days, a chain was thrown from a rock at one edge of the inlet to the opposite shore, as a barrier to hostile ships. This rock stands in the inlet today—appropriately named Chain Rock.

North of the Narrows stands Signal Hill, some 500 feet high, from which extends a marvelous panoramic view of the city of St. John's, the harbor, and out through the Narrows to the open Atlantic. Signal Hill is a most appropriate name, for from this hill, in 1901, Marconi sent his first successful trans-oceanic wireless message.

Many fine roads and highways traverse the Avalon Peninsula. From St. John's, north, splendid drives follow the seacoast. Spectacular marine scenery, sheer cliffs, picturesque fishing villages, dot the coastline at all points, particularly at Logy Bay, Outer Cove, Torbay, Flat Rock and Pouch Cove. This highway system continues around Conception Bay, turns north through Brigus, past Spaniard's Bay, Harbour Grace, and so on north to Bay de Verde. Another highway extends south of St. John's, along the coast toward Cape Race, while other roads traverse the region of Salmonier River to St. Mary's Bay and across to Placentia Bay.

However, as you travel to the west, highways are left behind. Transportation from the Avalon Peninsula to the west coast is dependent upon the Newfoundland Railway, which traverses the Island from St. John's on the extreme east, across the northern part of the great central portion of the Island and then swings to the southwest, through the Humber River country, past St. George's Bay and down the coast to end at the village of Port-Aux-Basques, at the extreme southwest tip of the Island. Naturally, transportation along the coast is primarily by boat, and throughout the summer, regular steamship service is maintained between St. John's and the Labrador coast, as well as between other coastal points. Throughout central and western Newfoundland, however, one is dependent primarily upon the Newfoundland Railway to reach the salmon rivers and lakes, and points of scenic interest.

From points on the rivers and lakes along the route of the railway, more distant points are accessible by means of trails through the forests, and by canoes and small boats on the rivers and lakes.

Along the extreme west coast, in the region of St. George's Bay, there are scattered bits of roadways, rapidly being connected and it probably will not be many years until western Newfoundland will have as good roads as the Avalon Peninsula now possesses. The visitor who comes by train or steamer to the busy industrial paper town of Corner Brook, on Humber Arm, is confronted with the amazing sight of apparently innumerable automobiles, all busily darting to and fro throughout the town. The questions naturally arise: Where did they come from? How did they get here? and Where do they go?

Perched high on its steep hillside commanding a magnificent view across Humber Arm, Corner Brook has a total of nine miles of streets within the town, and short scattered bits of roads, extending a little way out of town. Brought in by steamer, well over 500 automobiles traverse these nine miles of streets and roads, and a busy nine miles it is. One taxi driver, with many thousand miles on his speedometer, told me that he had circled and crisscrossed his own tracks so many times on that nine miles that he felt as though he were meeting himself every time he turned around.

Separated from other lands by many miles of forest and ocean, and far from major highways, I stopped short in amazement one morning, as I left the Glynmill Inn, the delightfully comfortable hostelry at Corner Brook, on my way down to the waterfront in search of pictures, on meeting a car with registration plates from my own home state.

It does not, however, require a great deal of imagination to picture the day, possibly not too far distant, when we shall be able to drive over beautiful highways to North Sydney, on the east coast of Cape Breton Island at the eastern tip of Nova Scotia, thence take our car by boat across to Port-Aux-Basques, and drive through the beautiful Little Codroy Valley, the Big Codroy, and on to the north past St. George's Bay, to Corner Brook and the Humber River country.

I think of this as one of the last outposts of vacation land to the northeast, and a glorious vacation land it will be. And looking still further into the future, it is not too difficult to visualize a highway continuing on across the great northern reaches of central Newfoundland, across the "barrens," and down to the Avalon Peninsula and the city of St. John's.

And then, too, who can say what part the airplane will play in the development of Newfoundland as a vacation land. Her coastal harbors and inland lakes are ideal landing-fields for amphibian planes; and Harbour Grace has long been the hopping-off point on the Avalon Peninsula for transatlantic flights. Whether from the utilitarian standpoint of transatlantic airways, or the more grim business of national defense—or from that of sports and pleasure-seeking vacationists in years to come, the Island Dominion is destined some day to have its place in the aviation sun.

But above all, Newfoundland is a sportsman's land. As Cod is King of the Sea, in this old Dominion-Colony of Britain, so Salmon is King of the River. Probably nowhere in the world today can the sportsman find salmon-fishing comparable to that in the innumerable rivers of Newfoundland that rise back in the hills and wind their way to the sea. All through western Newfoundland, in the Little Codroy, in the Big Codroy, in Robinson's River, in Fischell's, in Harry's River and especially in the Serpentine, will the salmon fisherman find sport to his heart's content. The Humber is probably the most famous and best-beloved salmon stream of all, for it is known to salmon fishermen the world over.

Many of these rivers emptying into the sea are also famous for sea trout. These trout, at about the season when salmon-fishing is at its best, come in from the sea and go up the rivers to spawn, as do the salmon. They provide splendid sport and can be caught in abundance.

Scattered over the length and breadth of Newfoundland, there are everywhere small ponds and tiny lakes, which literally teem with brown trout, and "trouting," as it is locally called, is much indulged in, and is the favorite sport of many who have neither the desire nor the time to venture further afield for sea trout and salmon.

In bygone years, caribou ranged over Newfoundland in uncounted thousands, sweeping across the "barrens" in their great migrations from north to south and back again, with the seasons. Hunted as mercilessly as were the buffalo herds of our own western plains, their ranks were decimated, until the caribou itself has as nearly reached the stage of extinction as did the bison. Now rigidly protected by law, however, this magnificent animal is staging a come-back and it is to be hoped that in years to come, caribou will again be found in abundance. It is the native deer of Newfoundland and, when you hear hunters and sportsmen speaking of "deer hunting," they are speaking of caribou, as there are no other native "deer" on the Island. Moose from Canada have been introduced in relatively recent years and are thriving and increasing in number, particularly in the heavily forested regions of the west coast.

In the fall of the year, local hunters go "partridge shooting" on the "barrens." The "partridge" of the Newfoundlander is the ptarmigan of the bird student. Belonging to the grouse and partridge family, the ptarmigan is a beautiful bird of the northland, which in summer is mottled gray and brown as the foliage, among which it feeds. With the coming of fall and winter, and the falling of snow and the accumulation of white snow patches on the ground, white patches begin to appear in the ptarmigan's plumage. By the time winter has set in and the land is white with snow, the ptarmigan has turned to pure white—one of Nature's greatest examples of caring for her children by means of protective coloration.

It is almost ten o'clock at night, as we stand on a high hill above the sea somewhere on the western coast. The sun is going down, a red-glowing ball of fire. Almost due north, it is sinking into the Straits of Belle Isle. A great play of streaming light and flaming color illumes the sky. Then it fades: there is a long dusky twilight, then at long last—near midnight—darkness.

As this northern summer night settles in utter stillness over us, there comes to us something of the spirit that must have prompted Sir Cavendish Boyle, once a governor of this British Dominion, to write

NEWFOUNDLAND

When sun-rays crown thy pine-clad hills,
And Summer spreads her hand,
When silvern voices tune thy rills,
We love thee, smiling land.
We love thee, we love thee,
We love thee, smiling land.

As loved our fathers, so we love,
Where once they stood, we stand;
Their prayer we raise to heav'n above:
God guard thee, Newfoundland,
God guard thee, God guard thee,
God guard thee, Newfoundland.

NEWFOUNDLAND
OUR NORTH DOOR NEIGHBOR

CARIBOU. The emblem of Newfoundland, the Caribou. Once ranging tundra and barren throughout the Island in vast herds, it became practically extinct. This is the bronze statue which stands in Bowring Park in the city of St. John's. *Page 33*

OUT OF THE NARROWS. Looking out to the wide Atlantic through the world-famous entrance to St. John's landlocked harbor. Signal Hill is on the left, with the fishermen's drying stages at its base. In the center of the channel is Chain Rock, to which the chain barriers used to be moored in time of war. *Page 34*

THE NARROWS FROM SIGNAL HILL. Looking to the south from the summit of Signal Hill. Approach to the city of St. John's by water can only be made through this narrow cleft in the coastline.

Page 35

THE HARBOR, ST. JOHN'S. Looking down upon the splendid landlocked harbor and the city of St. John's from the 500-foot summit of Signal Hill. Here Marconi in 1901 sent his first transoceanic radio message; and here each day comes the roar of the noon gun.

SUNLIT SHACKS. The Narrows at the foot of Signal Hill are lined with primitive drying stages and curing shacks for the omnipresent cod. At top right is Chain Rock.

LAST OF THE SEALERS. The remnants of the once great sealing fleet riding at anchor. The sealers used to throng St. John's and other Newfoundland ports in hundreds. Today, few remain. *Page 38*

ST. JOHN'S FROM ACROSS THE HARBOR. The skyline of the city from across the harbor, showing the impressive bulk of the Newfoundland Hotel to right of the center. Cosmopolitan shipping, large and small from all quarters of the globe, passes in and out of the harbor.

FRESH FISH, ST. JOHN'S. Countless tons of fish are handled on the piers of St. John's. Of dried fish alone, over 70,000 tons are shipped to the world market every year.

QUIDI VIDI. Known locally as Quidi Vidi Pond, this picturesque little landlocked sea-lake, lined with fish-curing stages, is close to St. John's, and attracts painters and photographers as well as devotees of water sports. *Page 41*

CASCADE GORGE. The road from St. John's to the south coast passes through wild and

OUTER COVE. Picturesque and characteristic fishing village a few miles north of St. John's. The drying and cleaning sheds and boats line the beach, and the fishermen's cottages scattered back from the sea. *Page 43*

LANDING STAGES. The catch is brought in by the boats, and men with pitchforks toss the fish from the boats to the lower stages. Caught there by another man with a fork, it is tossed on up to the next stage, and so on. *Page 44*

TORBAY. Only a few miles from St. John's, this is a typical one of the innumerable fishing villages scattered along the coast of the Avalon Peninsula. *Page 45*

SUNBURNED SONS OF THE SEA. Newfoundlanders are husky and hardy folk. These friendly young fishermen are showing twenty-pound cod, average specimens of their daily catch. *Page 46*

POUCH COVE. Another picturesque fishing village on the coast of the Avalon Peninsula, north of the city of St. John's. *Page 47*

FLAT ROCK. Hardy fishermen, sturdy youngsters and a trusty horse who all dwell in this tiny fishing village hidden between the perpendicular cliffs of the Avalon Peninsula.

Page 48

A ROCK-BOUND COAST. The Avalon Peninsula on the eastern shore is rugged and precipitous. Here and there amid the grim beauty of its forest-clad cliffs little coves give shelter from the fury of the open Atlantic. *Page 49*

LOGY BAY. Here is graphically shown the tenacious way in which the cleaning and

CLIFF WORKERS. Enlarged detail of the previous scene. Landing stage at bottom right is the spot from which the fish is hoisted to the precarious-looking sheds on the cliff top.

Page 51

A FISHERY ON STILTS. Another view of the same, giving an even better idea of this harsh and rock-bound coast that supplies so much dried codfish to the world. *Page 52*

ON THE "FLAKES." The crude log platforms on which the cod is cured after being cleaned and salted are called "flakes." Covered loosely with branches, the cod has to be constantly turned, stacked, re-spread or covered, as necessary, to avoid mildew from damp and over-dryness from the hot sun.

Page 53

"BUTTER POTS." These rocky outcrops along the highway from St. John's to Brigus, called locally "Butter Pots," are characteristic of the shore "barrens" round the end of Conception Bay. *Page 54*

TOPSAIL HIGHWAY. Topsail is a lovely vacation spot on Conception Bay. On the left can be seen the end of Bell Island, whose iron mines are among the largest in the world and extend far out under the sea.

TOPSAIL. Another view of the rocky coast, whose colorful cliffs, blue skies, blue-green water and green fields, combine to form out-of-the-world beauty and restfulness.

BATHING BEACH IN THE NORTHLAND. There are not many bathing beaches on Newfoundland's coast, for the water is chilly and the beaches are rough. Here is one, however, near Topsail, with the towering headland of Cape St. Francis in the far background.

SALMONIER RIVER. Its beauty and its salmon have made this one of Newfoundland's

BRIGUS AND THE "BARRENS." The "barrens" are vast areas of low-lying rocky hills along the edge of Conception Bay. They grow little but blueberries and wild strawberries. Brigus, nestling in its cove, is the home of Captain Bob Bartlett, the arctic explorer.

COASTLINE OF CONCEPTION BAY. The western edge of the great Conception Bay, not far from the village of Brigus. Neat fishermen's houses stand here and there—but there are still more weathered cellars and foundations of homes long since deserted and fallen to ruin.

Page 60

ENTRANCE TO BRIGUS HARBOR. Looking across the entrance to Brigus Harbor, and beyond, over the wide sweep of Conception Bay. *Page 61*

BRIGUS. Brigus is now but a shadow of its former self of the prosperous old sealing-days. The sailing of Captain Bob Bartlett on his schooner *The Morissey* is its major annual event. The Captain's house is under the trees in the right center of the picture. *Page 62*

A COVE ON GANDER LAKE. Gander Lake is one of the largest in the Island. Flowing from the south and west, Gander River flows into Gander Lake and out of it again on its way to the sea. *Page 63*

A BEAVER PROJECT. A beaver dam across a small stream, which, until recently, ran into Gander Lake. The industrious little animal-engineers have here managed to back up a sheet of shallow water three miles long. *Page 64*

BEAVER HOUSE, GANDER LAKE. Here is the home of a very active beaver colony in the Gander country. In the background are the forested, rolling hills of the interior of the Island, where hide the few remaining caribou. *Page 65*

DOWN THE BIG CHUTE, GANDER RIVER. Our Micmac guide, Jim, in his battered old canoe, starting to shoot the rapids of the Big Chute on Gander River. Jim knows every rock and every ledge in the swiftly rushing water. *Page 66*

SAIL UP! GANDER RIVER. After running the Big Chute rapids, Jim makes a sail out of his old brown blanket and a couple of fresh-cut spruce poles, so as to take advantage of the downstream wind.

Page 67

FULL SAIL AHEAD, GANDER RIVER. Here is Jim's blanket-sail in action, helping us to skim rapidly down the Gander River. *Page 68*

MICMAC STUDY. Close-up of Jim, a full-blooded Micmac, and our kindly and efficient guide-canoeist-cook, in the Gander country. The Micmacs are a branch of the Algonquins, and are scattered through Newfoundland and Canada's Eastern Provinces.

Page 69

SEA TROUT FROM THE GANDER RIVER. Averaging from two to four pounds each, sea trout, as they come up the rivers from the sea to spawn, provide splendid sport for the fishermen.

Page 70

A FINE MESS OF SEA TROUT. Just a part of an hour's catch on the Gander River. *Page 71*

GOING UP! Battling the rapids and the waterfalls, the salmon keep up their never-ending struggle to reach their spawning-grounds on the upper reaches of Newfoundland's rivers. Here is a big fellow making a mighty leap up a fall. *Page 72*

ACTION—HEAD ON! Nothing is more fascinating than to watch the salmon fighting their way up a rapid or a fall. This fellow, coming up through the torn water with terrific speed, is headed straight at the camera. *Page 73*

SUNSET ON GANDER RIVER. Summer days are long in Newfoundland. Photographs can often be taken from five in the morning until ten at night. Here is a spectacular cloud effect, taken from our camp at the close of a long day of fishing. *Page 74*

MARBLEHEAD AND THE HUMBER. Here, just above the village of Humbermouth, and just before emptying into the wide sea-inlet of Humber Arm, the Humber River sweeps smoothly and majestically round the base of the great crag known as Marblehead.

HILLS ALONG THE HUMBER. For mile upon mile your journey down the Humber takes you through the beautiful Humber Valley, where the magnificent river is flanked with forest-clad mountains. *Page 76*

A HUMBER HEADLAND, LIMESTONE QUARRY. Here the mighty Humber swings darkly and silently under the great headland known as Limestone Quarry, on which are the great quarries which supply the paper mills at Corner Brook with limestone. *Page 77*

TOMORROW'S NEWSPAPER! Uncounted cords of pulpwood, choking the course of the Humber, on their way to the ever-hungry paper mills at Corner Brook. *Page 78*

HUMBER REFLECTIONS. Here are the Steady Brook Falls tumbling out of the forest on a mountainside and reflected in the tranquil waters of the Humber River. *Page 79*

A CAMP ON THE HUMBER. A hunting camp among white birches on the bank of the Humber River.

Page 80

CORNER BROOK, BUSY TOWN! The busy pulp and paper center of Corner Brook, scattered over a hillside on Humber Arm. Over 500 local automobiles speed about the nine miles of streets in this far-off isolated industrial town. *Page 81*

PULP AT THE PAPER MILLS, CORNER BROOK. The great paper mills and the vast mountains of pulpwood at Corner Brook, the great paper-producing center of the Island. *Page 82*

MOUNT MARIA, NEAR CORNER BROOK. The rounded dome of old Mount Maria, near Corner Brook, is a familiar scene. To the right lies Humber Arm, long sea-inlet opening from Bay of Islands.

HUMBERMOUTH HILLS. Looking across Humber Arm towards the mouth of the Humber River.

Page 84

HUMBER ARM, TOWARDS BAY OF ISLANDS. Looking down the long reach of Humber Arm towards Bay of Islands, which is one of the most lovely scenic spots on Newfoundland's west coast.

Page 85

STORM OVER HUMBER ARM. A storm coming up over Humber Arm. In the center distance, on the other side of the Arm, the town of Corner Brook may be faintly seen through the rain that is beginning to sweep across the water. *Page 86*

DAWN, ON THE TRAIL TO THE SERPENTINE. Starting at dawn, with packers and guide, across the Great Swamp, on the way to the Serpentine River country. The railway, its nearest station at Spruce Brook, has been left far behind. *Page 87*

FERNS ON A FOREST TRAIL. The trail from Spruce Brook to the Serpentine River leads partly through dense virgin forest. Here is one of many great beds of shoulder-high ferns which we came upon. *Page 88*

PACKING TO THE SERPENTINE. A sturdy young Newfoundland packer on the trail. He is carrying a hundred pounds of supplies swung from a chest strap and a gunny sack across the forehead, and swings along, mile after mile, without a pause. *Page 89*

SERPENTINE LAKE. Serpentine Lake zigzags its course for seven miles through the mountains. Transportation is by means of a dory and an old river boat. This is a paradise for salmon fishers.

Page 90

TO FISH, OR NOT TO FISH! A pause on the banks of Serpentine Lake. Here the hills are only a few hundred feet high, the timber line still lower, and the flora and fauna subalpine in character.

Page 91

ALL ASHORE! SERPENTINE LAKE. Landing to make camp, at the lower end of the lake, isolated from the world by a ring of mountains. Serpentine River takes its rise here, and flows fifteen miles to the sea. *Page 92*

TWIN FALLS, CANYON BROOK. Canyon Brook is a small stream tumbling down the mountainside into Serpentine Lake. This is a hidden beauty spot we came upon.

Page 93

A LANDING, SERPENTINE RIVER. Getting ashore to build a fire, brew a pot of tea and rest for a spell, where every pool is a salmon rendezvous. *Page 94*

PORTAGE ON THE SERPENTINE. Portaging round a rough stretch of rapids on Serpentine River just above the Big Falls. It is late July, but there are still patches of snow here and there on the hills. *Page 95*

BIG FALLS OF THE SERPENTINE. The dull rumble of the falls is heard long before they are in sight. In the still pools below the falls is probably the best salmon-fishing in the Island.

Page 96

DESOLATE VALLEY OF THE SERPENTINE. Not a railway, not a road, not a trail, not a house is to be seen as we look down from a rocky height above the timber line down the uninhabited Valley of the Serpentine. *Page 97*

A STRIKE! DUSK ON THE SERPENTINE. As the sun goes down over the Serpentine, both the salmon and the fishermen bestir themselves. A strike, and the battle is on.

Page 98

END OF THE FIGHT. The battle is over, and the great fish, finally tired out by the expert skill of the angler, is brought to gaff. *Page 99*

HEADED FOR THE FRY PAN! The return to camp, with material for broiled salmon steaks for supper. Coffee, pipe, warm blankets on a bed of fir boughs, and the Serpentine to sing you to sleep!

Page 100

A DIFFICULT DECISION! One of life's greatest problems—which fly to use! a Discussion at Robinson's River, western Newfoundland. *Page 101*

LET'S TRY THIS ONE! At last a decision is reached, and we are ready for another try at the old "Big Fighter" who, so far, has been too much for us. *Page 102*

OFF FOR THE RIVER, ROBINSON'S. Leaving camp for the swift waters of Robinson's River, in a typical forest setting. *Page 103*

SETTLERS' CLEARINGS. Here are clearings in the virgin forest and settlers' houses built at the mouth of Robinson's River on the western coast of the Island. *Page 104*

A CORNUS CARPET. The Bunchberry *(Cornus canadensis)* is a cousin of the Dogwood, whose flowers it so much resembles. It carpets the Newfoundland forest-floors in lovely green and white profusion. *Page 105*

TOMORROW'S FOREST. A wagon road from village to railway station in western Newfoundland. The young spruce are beginning to encroach on it from both sides.

Page 106

HOME INDUSTRY. The little houses along the western Newfoundland shore are practically self-sufficient, what with fish, hens, pigs, a cow and the garden and fields. Here is a cottage-industry which helps—beautiful hooked rugs for use and for sale.
Page 107

VALE OF THE LITTLE CODROY. The Little Codroy is one of the most beautiful valleys in all Newfoundland. Calm and peaceful, a perfect garden spot for a vacation.

Page 108

PEACEFUL VALLEY. Looking down the Little Codroy Valley, towards Port-aux-Basques. The fertile meadows are flanked by the rolling ranges of the Cape Anguille Mountains. *Page 109*

WHEN DAY IS DONE! The guide beaches his canoe for the night as darkness begins to settle over lake and forest.

Page 110

GATHERING STORM. Summer storms arise quickly in the north, and with equal suddenness give way to brilliant sunshine. Here is a heavy squall gathering over St. George's Lake in western Newfoundland.

Page 111

LAKE AND SNOW. Another lake on the western coast, showing the black hills and the dark forests—to say nothing of snow-patches still unmelted in July. *Page 112*

GRIM, DARK HILLS. Here the grim hills, the dark forest, the cloud-filled sky make a picture typical of the wild and rugged charm of the western coast. *Page 113*

WILD IRIS. Here on the sandy flats at the mouth of a small river on the western coast, are acres upon acres of Wild Iris blooming in profusion. *Page 114*

PLACENTIA. Two hundred and eighty years ago Placentia was an armed stronghold of the French in their wars against the British. Now, after two centuries of sleepy, peaceful fishing-village life it is in the headlines, selected as the site for an air base in a gigantic defense program. *Page 115*

LONG ARM OF THE SEA. This is not a river. It is Southeast Arm, one of the narrow meandering sea-inlets which indent the southern coast of the Island. Placentia is on the other side of the mountains in the background. *Page 116*